THIS NOTEBOOK BELONGS TO

Made in the USA
Monee, IL
19 December 2021

86396998R00056